A Rulebook
for Arguments

Anthony Weston

A Rulebook
for Arguments

Hackett Publishing Company
Indianapolis & Cambridge

Printed in the United States of America

For further information, please address
  Hackett Publishing Company
  P.O. Box 44937
  Indianapolis, Indiana 46204

91   90   6   5

Library of Congress Cataloging-in-Publication Data

Weston, Anthony, 1954–
    A rulebook for arguments.

    "An Avatar book."
    Bibliography: p.
    1. Reasoning.   2. Logic   3. English language–
Rhetoric.   I. Title.
BC177.W47   1987   168   86-25899
ISBN 0-87220-030-2
ISBN 0-87220-029-9 (pbk.)

Contents

Preface

This book is a brief introduction to the art of writing
and assessing arguments. It sticks to the bare essentials.
I have found that students and writers often need just
such a list of reminders and rules, not lengthy introductory explanations; thus, unlike most textbooks in argumentative writing or "informal logic," this book is
organized around specific rules, illustrated and
explained soundly but above all briefly. It is not a text-
book but a *rule*book.

Instructors too, I have found, often wish to assign
such a rulebook, a treatment which students can consult
and understand on their own and which therefore does
not intrude on classtime. Here again it is important to be
brief—the point is to help students get on with writing a
paper or with assessing an argument—but the rules must
be stated with enough explanation that an instructor can
simply refer a student to "rule 13" or "rule 23" rather
than writing an entire explanation in the margins of each
student's paper. Brief but self-sufficient: that is the fine
line I have tried to follow.

This rulebook can also be used in a course that gives
explicit attention to arguments. It will need to be supplemented with exercises and with more examples, but

there are many texts already available which consist
largely or wholly of such exercises and examples. *Those*
texts, however, also need to be supplemented—with what
this rulebook offers: simple rules for putting good arguments together. Too many students come out of "informal logic" courses knowing only how to shoot down (or
at least *at*) selected fallacies. Too often they are unable
to explain what is actually wrong, or to launch an argument of their own. Informal logic can do better: this
book is one attempt to suggest how.

Comments and criticisms are welcome.

Anthony Weston
Department of Philosophy
State University of New York
Stony Brook, New York 11794

August, 1986

Introduction

What's the Point of Arguing?

Some people think that arguing is simply stating their prejudices in a new form. This is why many people also think that arguments are unpleasant and pointless. One dictionary definition for "argument" is "disputation." In this sense we sometimes say that two people "*have* an argument": a verbal fistfight. It happens often enough. But it is not what arguments really are.

In this book, "to give an argument" means *to offer a set of reasons or evidence in support of a conclusion.* Here an argument is *not* simply a statement of certain views, and it is not simply a dispute. Arguments are attempts to *support* certain views with reasons. Nor are arguments in this sense pointless: in fact, they are essential.

Argument is essential, in the first place, because it is a way of trying to find out which views are better than others. Not all views are equal. Some conclusions can be supported by good reasons; others have much weaker support. But often we don't know which are which. We need to give arguments for different conclusions and then assess those arguments to see how strong they really are.

Argument in this sense is a means of *inquiry.* Some philosophers and activists have argued, for instance, that the "factory farming" of animals for meat causes immense suffering to animals and is therefore unjustified and immoral. Are they right? You can't tell by consulting your prejudices. Many issues are involved. Do we have moral obligations to other species, for instance, or is only human suffering really bad? How well can humans live without meat? Some vegetarians have lived to very old ages. Does this show that vegetarian diets are healthier? Or is it irrelevant when you consider that some nonvegetarians have also lived to very old ages? (You might make some progress by asking whether a higher *percentage* of vegetarians live to old age.) Or might healthy people tend to become vegetarians, rather than vice versa? All of these questions need to be considered carefully, and the answers are not clear in advance.

Argument is essential for another reason too. Once we have arrived at a conclusion that is well-supported by reasons, argument is the way in which we explain and *defend* it. A good argument doesn't merely repeat conclusions. Instead it offers reasons and evidence, so that other people can make up their minds for themselves. If you become convinced that we should indeed change the way we raise and use animals, for example, you must use arguments to explain how you arrived at your conclusion: that is how you will convince others. Offer the reasons and evidence that convinced *you*. It is not a mistake to have strong views: the mistake is to have nothing else.

Understanding Argumentative Essays

The rules of argument, then, are not arbitrary: they have a specific purpose. But students (as well as other writers) do not always understand that purpose when first assigned argumentative essays—and if you don't understand an assignment you are unlikely to do well on it. Many students, asked to argue for their views on some issue, write out elaborate *statements* of their views but do not offer any real *reasons* to think that their views are correct. They write an essay, but not an argumentative one.

This is a natural misunderstanding. In high school, the emphasis is on learning subjects which are fairly clearcut and uncontroversial. You need not *argue* that the United States Constitution provides for three branches of government, or that Shakespeare wrote *Macbeth*. These are facts that you only need to master, and that your papers only need to report.

Students come to college expecting more of the same. But many college courses—especially those that assign writing— have a different aim. These courses are concerned with the *basis* of our beliefs; they require students to *question* their beliefs and to work out and defend their own views. The issues discussed in college courses are often those issues which are *not* so clearcut and certain. Yes, the Constitution provides for three branches of government, but should the Supreme Court really have veto power over the other two? Yes, Shakespeare wrote *Macbeth*, but what did he mean by it? Reasons and evidence can be given for different answers. Students in these courses are asked to learn to think for themselves, to form their own views in a responsible way. The ability to *defend* your views is a measure of that skill, and that is why argumentative essays are so important.

In fact, as Chapters VII–IX will explain, to write a good argumentative essay you must use arguments *both* as a means of inquiry *and* as a way of explaining and defending your conclusions. You must prepare for the paper by exploring the arguments on the opposing sides; then you must write the essay itself as an argument, defending your conclusions with arguments and critically assessing some of the arguments on the opposing sides.

Outline of This Book

This book begins by discussing fairly simple arguments and moves to argumentative essays at the end.

Chapters I–VI are about composing and assessing *short* arguments. A "short" argument simply offers its reasons and evidence briefly, usually in a few sentences or a paragraph. We begin with short arguments for several reasons. First, they are common. In fact they are so common that they are part of every day's conversation. Second, long arguments are often elaborations of short arguments, and/or series of short arguments linked together. Learn to write and assess short arguments first; then you will be able to extend your skills to argumentative essays.

A third reason for beginning with short arguments is that they are the best illustrations both of the common argument forms and of the typical mistakes in arguments. In long arguments it is harder to pick out the main points—and the main problems. Although some of the rules may seem obvious when first stated, then, remember that you have the benefit of a simple example. Other rules are hard enough to appreciate even in short arguments.

Chapters VII, VIII, and IX turn to argumentative essays. Chapter VII is about the first step: exploring the issue. Chapter VIII outlines the main points of an argumentative essay; Chapter IX adds rules specifically about writing it. All of these chapters depend on Chapters I–VI, since an argumentative essay essentially combines and elaborates the kinds of short arguments that Chapters I–VI discuss. Don't skip ahead to the argumentative essay chapters, then, even if you come to this book primarily for help writing an essay. The book is short enough to read through to Chapters VII, VIII, and IX, and when you arrive there you will have the tools you need to use those chapters well. Instructors might

Maybe your idea is that being an optimist gives you more energy to work for success, whereas pessimists feel defeated in advance, and therefore never even try. Thus you have one main premise: optimists are more likely to succeed, to achieve their goals. (Maybe this is what Churchill meant as well.) If this *is* your premise, say so explicitly.

Once you have finished this book, you will have a convenient list of many of the different forms that arguments can take. Use them to develop your premises. To defend a generalization, for instance, check Chapter II; it will remind you that you need to give a series of examples as premises, and it will tell you what sorts of examples to look for. If your conclusion requires a "deductive" argument like those explained in Chapter VI, the rules discussed in that chapter will tell you what premises you need. You may have to try several different arguments before you find one which works well.

(2) Present your ideas in a natural order

Short arguments are usually written in one or two paragraphs. Put the conclusion first, followed by your reasons, or set out your premises first and draw the conclusion at the end. In any case, set out your ideas in an order that unfolds your line of thought most naturally for the reader. Consider this short argument by Bertrand Russell:

> The evils of the world are due to moral defects quite as much as to lack of intelligence. But the human race has not hitherto discovered any method of eradicating moral defects ... Intelligence, on the contrary, is easily improved by methods known to every competent educator. Therefore, until some method of teaching virtue has been discovered,

progress will have to be sought by improvement of intelligence rather than of morals.*

Each claim in this passage leads naturally to the next. Russell begins by pointing out the two sources of evil in the world: "moral defects," as he puts it, and lack of intelligence. He then claims that we do not know how to correct "moral defects," but that we do know how to correct lack of intelligence. Therefore—notice that the word "therefore" clearly marks his conclusion—progress will have to come by improving intelligence.

Each sentence in this argument is in just the right place. Plenty of wrong places were available. Suppose Russell instead wrote it like this:

> The evils of the world are due to moral defects quite as much as lack of intelligence. Until some method of teaching virtue has been discovered, progress will have to be sought by improvement of intelligence rather than of morals. Intelligence is easily improved by methods known to every competent educator. But the human race has not hitherto discovered any means of eradicating moral defects.

These are exactly the same premises and conclusion, but they are in a different order, and the word "therefore" has been omitted before the conclusion. Now the argument is *much* harder to understand: the premises do not fit together naturally, and you have to read the passage twice just to figure out what the conclusion is. Don't count on your readers to be so patient.

Expect to rearrange your argument several times to find the most natural order. The rules discussed in this book will also help: you can use them not only to tell

---

Skeptical Essays (London: Allen and Unwin, 1977), p. 127.

what premises you need, but also how to arrange your premises in the most natural order.

(3) Start from reliable premises

No matter how well you argue *from* premises to conclusion, your conclusion will be weak if your premises are weak.

> Nobody in the world today is really happy. Therefore, it seems that human beings are just not made for happiness. Why should we expect what we can never find?

The premise of this argument is the statement that nobody in the world today is really happy. Ask yourself if this premise is plausible. Is *nobody* in the world today really happy? At the very least this premise needs some defense, and very likely it is just not true. This argument cannot show, then, that human beings are not made for happiness, or that we should not expect to be happy.

Sometimes it is easy to start from reliable premises. You may have well-known examples at hand, or informed authorities who are clearly in agreement. Other times it is harder. If you are not sure about the reliability of a premise, you may need to do some research, and/or give a short argument for the premise itself. We will return to this in later chapters, especially in section A2 of Chapter VII. If you find that you *cannot* argue adequately for your premise(s), then, of course, you need to give up entirely and start elsewhere!

(4) Use definite, specific, concrete language

Write concretely: avoid abstract, vague, general terms. "We hiked for hours in the sun" is a hundred times better than "It was an extended period of laborious exertion."

NO:

> For those whose roles primarily involved the performance of services, as distinguished from assumption of leadership responsibilities, the main pattern seems to have been a response to the leadership's invoking obligations that were concomitants of the status of membership in the societal community and various of its segmental units. The closest modern analogy is the military service performed by an ordinary citizen, except that the leader of the Egyptian bureaucracy did not need a special emergency to invoke legitimate obligations.*

YES:

> In ancient Egypt the common people were liable to be conscripted for work.

(5) Play fair

Do not make your argument look good by caricaturing the opposing side. Generally people advocate a position for serious and sincere reasons. Try to figure out their view, even if you think they are dead wrong. A person who opposes the use of a new technology is not necessarily in favor of "going back to the caves," for example, and a person who advocates reduced military spending

---

*This passage is from Talcott Parsons, *Societies: Evolutionary and Comparative Perspectives*, p. 56. I owe the quotation and the rewritten version which follows to Stanislas Andreski, *Social Sciences as Sorcery* (New York: St Martin's Press, 1972), Chapter 6.

is not necessarily in favor of "giving in to the Russians." If you can't imagine how anyone could hold the view you are attacking, you just don't understand it yet.

In general, avoid language whose *only* function is to sway the emotions of your readers or hearers, either for or against the view you are discussing. This is "loaded" language.

> Electoral sabotage played an important role in the secret war in Brazil. The CIA invested some $20 million to finance conservatives in the ... Brazilian election. The money was used to buy candidates in eight of eleven gubernatorial elections ...*

Here the summary term "war" is itself loaded: military involvement is not alleged. "Sabotage" and "buy" are also inappropriate. An election might be truly "sabotaged" if ballot boxes throughout the country were stuffed, and an official might be "bought" if he or she were paid to vote as directed. In this excerpt, however, the CIA is accused only of giving money to conservative candidates in the election. It is not clear that anyone is "bought" merely by covert campaign contributions —especially if he or she is already committed to the point of view the CIA favors. Thus the summary sentence should read:

> The CIA tried to influence the Brazilian election by giving money to conservative candidates.

The neutralized statement does not excuse the CIA's involvement. On the contrary, it now should be taken all the more seriously. Loaded language preaches only to

---

*"The Secret War in Brazil," *The Progressive*, August 1977.

the converted, but careful presentation of the facts can itself convert.

(6) Use consistent terms

Stick to a single set of terms for each idea. If you want to argue that Senator Gunderson's views are liberal, then use the word "liberal" in your premises, not (or not just) words like "left-leaning" or "in the New Deal tradition."

Consistent terms are especially important when your argument depends on the connections between the premises.

NO:

> If you study other cultures, then you realize what a variety of human customs there is. If you understand the diversity of social practices, then you question your own customs. If you acquire doubts about the way you do things, then you become more tolerant. Therefore, if you expand your knowledge of anthropology, then you become more likely to accept other people and practices without criticism.

YES:

> If you study other cultures, then you realize what a variety of human customs there is. If you realize what a variety of human customs there is, then you question your own customs. If you question your own customs, then you become more tolerant. Therefore, if you study other cultures, then you become more tolerant.

In both versions, each of the sentences has the form "If X, then Y." In the second version, though, the "Y" of the first statement is exactly the "X" of the second, the

"Y" of the second is exactly the "X" of the third, and so on. (Go back and look.) This is why the second argument is easy to read and to understand: it forms a kind of chain. In the first version, the "Y" of the first statement is only roughly the "X" of the second, the "Y" of the second statement only roughly the "X" of the third, and so on. Here each "X" and "Y" is written as if the author had consulted a thesaurus at every opportunity. "More tolerant" in the third sentence, for instance, is written as "more likely to accept other people and practices without criticism" in the conclusion. As a result, the tight *connection* between the individual premises, and between the premises and the conclusion, is lost. The writer shows off, but the reader—who is not privileged to know the structure of the argument from the start—is left to flounder.

Also, avoid using markers like "the former" and "the latter." Usually your readers must stop, look back, and puzzle out what "the former" and "the latter" *are* in each case. Repeat the phrases. The former is quicker, but the latter is almost always clearer.

(7) Stick to one meaning for each term

The opposite temptation is to use a single word in more than one sense. This is the classical fallacy of "equivocation."

> Women and men are physically and emotionally different. The sexes are *not* "equal," then, and therefore the law should not pretend that we are!

This argument may seem plausible at first glance, but it plays on two different senses of "equal." It is true that the sexes are not physically and emotionally "equal," in the sense in which "equal" means simply "identical."

"Equality" before the *law*, however, does not mean "physically and emotionally identical," but rather "entitled to the same rights and opportunities." Rephrased, then, with the two different senses of "equal" made clear, the argument goes:

> Women and men are not physically and emotionally identical. Therefore, women and men are not entitled to the same rights and opportunities.

This version of the argument no longer equivocates on "equal," but it is still not a good argument; it is only the original inadequate argument with the inadequacy no longer hidden. Once the equivocation is removed, it becomes clear that the conclusion of the argument is neither supported by or even related to the premise. No reason is offered to show that physical and emotional differences should have anything to do with rights and opportunities.

Sometimes we are tempted to equivocate by making a key word *vague*. Consider the following conversation:

> A: Everyone is really just selfish!
>
> B: But what about John: look how he devotes himself to his children!
>
> A: He is only doing what he really wants to do: that's still selfish!

Here the meaning of "selfish" changes from A's first claim to A's second. In the first claim, we understand "selfish" to mean something fairly specific: the grasping, self-centered behavior we ordinarily call "selfish." In A's response to B's objection, A expands the meaning of "selfish" to include apparently unselfish behavior too, by broadening the definition to just "doing what you really want to do." A saves only the *word*; it has lost its original, specific meaning.

A good way to avoid equivocation is to carefully *define* any key terms when you introduce them: then be sure to use them only as you've defined them! You may also need to define special terms or technical words. Use definite, specific, and concrete language in your definitions (rule 4), and avoid loaded language (rule 5). Notice that dictionary definitions carefully avoid loaded terms. "Abortion" is defined in my *Webster's* simply as "the forcible expulsion of the mammalian fetus prematurely, especially at any time before it is viable." Whether abortion is moral or immoral is not up to the dictionary.

II

Arguments by Example

Arguments by example offer one or more specific examples in support of a generalization.

> Women in earlier times were married very young. Juliet in Shakespeare's *Romeo and Juliet* was not even fourteen. In the Middle Ages the Jewish *Mishna* regarded thirteen as the normal age of marriage for a girl. And during the Roman Empire many Roman women were married while thirteen or younger.

This argument generalizes from three examples—Juliet, Jewish women in the Middle Ages, and Roman women during the Roman Empire—to *many* or *most* women in earlier times. To see the form of this argument most clearly, we can list the premises separately, with the conclusion on the "bottom line":

> Juliet in Shakespeare's play was not even fourteen.
>
> Jewish women during the Middle Ages were normally married at thirteen.
>
> Many Roman women during the Roman Empire were married while thirteen or younger.
>
> Therefore, many women in earlier times were married very young.

I will often write short arguments in this way when it is important to see exactly how they work.

When do premises like these adequately support a generalization?

One requirement, of course, is that the examples be accurate. Remember rule 3: an argument must start from reliable premises! If Juliet *wasn't* around fourteen, or if most Roman or Jewish women *weren't* married at thirteen or younger, then the argument is much weaker, and if none of the premises can be supported, there is no argument at all. To check an argument's examples, or to find good examples for your own arguments, you may need to do some research.

But suppose that the examples *are* accurate. Generalizing from them is still a tricky business. Chapter II offers a short checklist for assessing arguments by example—both your own and others'.

(8) Is there more than one example?

A single example can sometimes be used for the sake of *illustration*. The example of Juliet alone might illustrate early marriage. But a single example offers next to no *support* for a generalization. It may be an atypical case, the "exception which proves the rule." More than one example is needed.

NO:

The right of women to vote was won only after a struggle.

Therefore, all women's rights are won only after struggles.

YES:

The right of women to vote was won only after a struggle.

The right of women to attend colleges and universities was won only after a struggle.

The right of women to equal employment opportunity is being won only with a struggle.

The Equal Rights Amendment will be passed, if at all, only after a struggle.

Therefore, all women's rights are won only after struggles.

In a generalization about a relatively small set of things, the best argument considers all, or nearly all, the examples. A generalization about all American presidents since World War II should consider each of them in turn. Likewise, the argument that women's rights have always required struggles should consider all, or most, important rights.

Generalizations about larger sets of things require picking out a "sample." We certainly cannot list all women in earlier times who married young; instead, our argument must offer a few women as examples of the rest. How many examples are required depends partly on their representativeness, a point that section 9 takes up. It also depends partly on the size of the set being generalized about. Large sets usually require more examples. The claim that your town is full of remarkable people requires more evidence than the claim that, say, your *friends* are remarkable people. Depending on how many friends you have, even just two or three examples might be enough to establish that your friends are remarkable people, but unless your town is very, very small, many more examples are required to show that your town is full of remarkable people.

(9) Are the examples representative?

Even a large number of examples may *misrepresent* the set being generalized about. A large number of examples of Roman women alone, for example, might establish very little about women generally, since Roman women are not necessarily representative of women in other parts of the world. The argument needs to consider women from other parts of the world as well.

> Everyone in my neighborhood favors McGraw for President.
>
> Therefore, McGraw is sure to win.

This argument is weak because single neighborhoods seldom represent the voting population as a whole. A well-to-do neighborhood may favor a candidate who is unpopular with everyone else. Student wards in university towns regularly are carried by candidates who do poorly elsewhere. Also, we seldom have good evidence even about neighborhood views. The set of people who put signs in their yards and stickers on their cars (and whose lawns are visible from busy roads or who drive regularly and/or park their cars in noticeable locations) may well misrepresent the neighborhood as a whole.

A *good* argument that "McGraw is sure to win" requires a representative sample of the entire voting population. It is not easy to construct such a sample. Public-opinion polls, for instance, construct their samples very carefully. They learned the hard way. In 1936, the *Literary Digest* conducted the first large-scale public opinion poll, predicting the outcome of the Presidential contest between Roosevelt and Landon. Names were taken, as they are now, from telephone listings, and also from automobile registration lists. The number of people polled was certainly not too small: more than two million "ballots" were counted. The poll predicted a wide victory for Landon. Roosevelt, however, won easily. In retrospect it is easy to see what went wrong. In 1936 only a select portion of the population owned telephones and automobiles. The sample was sharply biased toward wealthy and urban voters, more of whom supported Landon.*

Polls have improved since then. Nonetheless, there are worries about the representativeness of their samples, particularly when the samples are fairly small. Nearly everyone now has a telephone, to be sure, but some people have more than one; many others have unlisted numbers; some numbers represent a whole household of voters and others only one; some people are less likely to be home to answer the phone; and so on. Even carefully selected samples, then, may be unrepresentative. Many of the best polls, for instance, badly miscalled the 1980 Presidential election.

The representativeness of any given sample, then, is always somewhat uncertain. Anticipate this danger! Look for samples that represent the whole population being generalized about. Do not survey only your friends or your neighborhood, and do not accept someone else's argument if it is based on such a survey. A survey of student attitudes, for instance, shouldn't limit the sample to, say, students coming out of movies on Friday night. A random sampling of student names from the student directory is required, and even this may not produce an entirely representative sample, because some students may be too busy, or too uninterested, or too offended, to respond.

---

*Mildred Parten, *Surveys, Polls, and Samples* (New York: Harper and Row, 1950), pp. 25, 290, 393f. Parten shows that lower income people, who were less likely to receive "ballots" than wealthy people, were also less likely to return their "ballot."

Do some research. Juliet, for example, is just one woman. Is she representative even of women in her time and place? Use your library! In Shakespeare's play, for example, Juliet's mother says to her:

> Think of marriage now; younger than you,
> Here in Verona, ladies of esteem,
> Are made already mothers. By my count,
> I was your mother much upon these years
> That you are now a maid ... (I, *iii*, 69–73)

This passage suggests that Juliet's marriage at fourteen is not exceptional: in fact, at fourteen, she seems to be a little on the old side.

When making your own argument, do not rely only on examples that come "off the top of your head." The sorts of examples you are likely to think of at a moment's notice are likely to be biased. Again, do some reading, think about the appropriate sample carefully, and keep yourself honest by looking for counterexamples (rule 11).

(10) Background information is crucial

We often need *background information* before we can assess a set of examples.

NO:

> You should use Slapdash Services—we already have dozens of completely satisfied customers in your area!

Slapdash may indeed have "dozens" of "completely" satisfied customers in your area—although this sort of claim is often made without any evidence at all—but you also need to consider how many people in your area have *tried* Slapdash. If a thousand people have tried Slapdash, and two dozen are satisfied, then, although there are indeed "dozens" of satisfied customers, Slapdash satisfies only 2.4% of its customers. Try somewhere else.

BETTER:

> You should use Slapdash Services—of the forty people in your area who have tried Slapdash, more than two dozen have been completely satisfied.

Here at least you can begin to assess the "dozens" statistic: Slapdash appears to satisfy more than 50% of the time. However, the argument is still unacceptably vague ("more than" two dozen, "completely satisfied ..."), and the representativeness of the forty people who have used Slapdash is not clear either. Arguments like these require careful detail, which advertisements seldom offer.

Or again:

> The "Bermuda Triangle" area off Bermuda is famous as a place where many ships and planes have mysteriously disappeared. There have been several dozen disappearances in the last decade alone.

No doubt. But "several dozen" out of how many ships and planes that *passed through* the area? Several dozen, or several tens of thousands? If only several dozen have disappeared out of (say) 20,000, then the disappearance rate in the Bermuda Triangle may well be normal, or even low.

Consider how often, when buying a car or selecting a school, we are swayed by the reports of a few friends or one or two experiences of our own. Hearing about someone's sister-in-law who had a terrible time with her Volvo is enough to keep many of us from buying a Volvo—even though *Consumer Reports* might indicate that Volvos are generally very reliable cars. We let one vivid example outweigh the careful summary and comparison of thousands of repair records. Richard Nisbett and Lee Ross term this the "person who" argument,* as in "I know a *person who* smoked three packs of cigarettes a day and lived to be 100" or "I know a *person who* had a Volvo that was a real lemon." It is nearly always a fallacy. As Nisbett and Ross point out, one car that turns out to be a lemon only changes the frequency-of-repair records slightly.

To judge an enumeration of examples, then, we often need to consider background *rates*. Correspondingly, when an argument offers rates or percentages, the relevant background information usually must include the *number* of examples. Car thefts on campus may have increased 100%, but if this means that two cars were stolen rather than one, not much has changed. This mistake too is common. Suppose my salary increases only 5% while yours increases 50%. It sounds unfair. If I started out making $50,000, though, and you started out making $5,000, then I am now getting $52,500 and you are now getting $7,500, and it's certainly not clear that I have any reason to complain.

One last example. An article arguing that the United States was behind a coup in Brazil claims that

> after the coup, foreign investments quickly poured in . . .
> Four years after the coup, foreign capital had seized control

---

*See *Human Inference: Strategies and Shortcomings of Social Judgment* (Englewood Cliffs, NJ: Prentice-Hall, 1980), p. 61. Actually they call it the "man who" argument; I have neutralized the language.

of the private sector: 100% of the automobile and tire production, 90% of cement, 80% of the pharmaceutical industry, 60% of the auto parts factories, and more than 50% of
chemical and machinery production.*

Impressive numbers. They *begin* to show that foreign
investment (notice, not specifically American) domi-
nates certain sectors of the Brazilian economy, although
we are not told how important any of these sectors are in
the overall picture. But these numbers are *entirely useless*
for showing that "foreign investments quickly poured
in," for the simple reason that no *pre*-coup figures are
offered at all. Without that background information,
there is no way of knowing whether foreign capital's
control of 80% of the pharmaceutical industry, for
instance, represents an increase or a decrease. For all we
know foreign investment might even have *declined!*

(11) Are there counterexamples?

Check generalizations by asking if there are counterexamples.

> The Peloponnesian War was caused by the Athenians'
> and Spartans' desire to dominate Greece.
>
> The Napoleonic Wars were caused by Napoleon's desire
> to dominate Europe.
>
> World War Two was caused by the Fascists' desire to
> dominate Europe.
>
> Thus, in general, wars are caused by the desire for terri-
> torial domination.

---

*"The Secret War in Brazil," *The Progressive*, August 1977.

Are *all* wars, however, caused by the desire for territorial domination? Or is the generalization perhaps too broad? In fact, there are counterexamples. Revolutions, for example, have quite different causes. So do civil wars.

If you can think of counterexamples to a generalization that you want to defend, revise your generalization. If the above argument were yours, for instance, you might change the conclusion to "Wars *between independent states* are caused by the desire for territorial domination." Even this may overgeneralize, but it is at least a more defensible conclusion than the original.

Other times you may want to dispute the supposed counterexample. World War I, someone may object, seems to have been caused not by the desire for territorial domination, but by a network of mutual defense pacts and other political intrigues, by the restlessness of the European upper classes, by the nationalist unrest in Eastern Europe, and so on. In the face of this example, you might of course give up your claim entirely, or weaken it still further. Another response, however, is to argue that the supposed counterexample actually does conform to the generalization. After all (you might argue), the desires of the European powers to dominate Europe were the *motives* for the mutual defense pacts and other intrigues which finally set off the war. And might not nationalist unrest too be caused by unjust domination presently in place? Here, in effect, you try to reinterpret the *counter*example as another *example*; the initial challenge to your conclusion becomes another piece of evidence for it. You may or may not change the phrasing of your conclusion: in any case you yourself now understand your claim better, and you are prepared to answer an important objection.

Also try to think of counterexamples when you are assessing someone else's arguments. Ask whether *their* conclusions might have to be revised and limited, whether perhaps those conclusions might have to be given up entirely, or whether a supposed counterexample might be reinterpreted as another example. The same rules apply to anyone else's arguments as apply to yours; the only difference is that you have a chance to correct your overgeneralizations yourself.

III

Arguments by Analogy

There is an exception to rule 8 ("Use more than one example"). *Arguments by analogy*, rather than multiplying examples to support a generalization, argue from *one* specific case or example to another example, reasoning that because the two examples are alike in many ways they are also alike in one further specific way.

> Vice-President George Bush once argued that the Vice-President's role is to support the President's policies, whether or not he or she agrees with them, because "You don't tackle your own quarterback."

Bush is suggesting that being part of an Administration is like being part of a football team. When you join a football team, you agree to abide by the decisions of the quarterback, because the team's success depends on obedience. Similarly, Bush suggests, joining the Administration is a commitment to abide by the decisions of the President, because the success of the Administration also depends on obedience. Distinguishing premises and conclusion:

> When you join a football team, you agree to abide by the decisions of the quarterback (because the team's success depends on the obedience of its members).
>
> A Presidential Administration is *like* a football team (its success too depends on the obedience of its members).
>
> Therefore, when you join a Presidential Administration, you agree to abide by the decisions of the President.

Notice that I have italicized the word "like" in the second premise. When an argument stresses the likeness between two cases, it is very probably an argument from analogy.

Here is a more complex example.

> An interesting switch was pulled in Rome yesterday by Adam Nordwell, an American Chippewa chief. As he descended his plane from California dressed in full tribal regalia, Nordwell announced in the name of the American Indian people that he was taking possession of Italy "by right of discovery" in the same way that Christopher Columbus did in America. "I proclaim this day the day of the discovery of Italy," said Nordwell. "What right did Columbus have to discover America when it had already been inhabited for thousands of years? The same right I now have to come to Italy and proclaim the discovery of your country."*

Nordwell is suggesting that his "discovery" of Italy is *like* Columbus's "discovery" of America in at least one important way: both Nordwell and Columbus claimed a country which had already been inhabited by its own people for centuries. Thus Nordwell insists that he has as much "right" to claim Italy as Columbus had to claim

---

Miami News 9/23/73.

America. But, of course, Nordwell has no right at all to claim Italy. Therefore Columbus had no right at all to claim America.

> Nordwell has no right to claim Italy for another people, let alone "by right of discovery" (since Italy has been inhabited by its own people for centuries).
>
> Columbus's claim to America "by right of discovery" is *like* Nordwell's claim to Italy (America too had been inhabited by its own people for centuries).
>
> Therefore, Columbus had no right to claim America for another people, let alone "by right of discovery."

How do we evaluate arguments by analogy?

The first premise of an argument by analogy makes a claim about the example used as an analogy. Remember rule 3: make sure that this premise is true. Is it true that Nordwell has no right to claim Italy for the Chippewa Indians? (Yes.) Is it true that when you join a football team you agree to abide by the decisions of the quarterback? (More or less: but you might *want* to tackle your own quarterback if he is running toward the wrong goal!)

The second premise in arguments by analogy claims that the example in the first premise is *like* the example about which the argument draws a conclusion. Evaluating this premise is harder, and needs a rule of its own.

(12) *Analogy requires a relevantly similar example*

Analogies do not require that the example used as an analogy be *just* like the example in the conclusion. A Presidential Administration is not just like a football

team. The Administration is made up of thousands of
people, for instance, while a football team involves thirty
or forty. Analogies require only *relevant* similarities. The
size of the team is irrelevant to Bush's point: the point is
about what teamwork requires.

One *relevant* difference between a football team and a
Presidential Administration is that in a football game
everything depends on thinking and acting quickly,
whereas normally the decisions of an Administration
should be taken with care and deliberation. This difference is relevant because when there is time for deliberation it may be important for the Vice-President to speak
up if he or she disagrees with the President. Bush's analogy, then, is only partly successful.

Likewise, twentieth-century Italy is not just like
fifteenth-century America. Italy is known to every twentieth-century schoolchild, for instance, whereas in the
fifteenth century America was unknown to much of the
world. Nordwell is not an explorer, and a commercial jet
is not the *Santa Maria*. Nordwell suggests, however, that
these differences are not relevant to the analogy.
Nordwell simply means to remind us that it is senseless
to claim a country that is already inhabited by its own
people. Whether that land is known to the world's
schoolchildren, or how the "discoverer" arrived there, is
not important. The more appropriate reaction might be
to try to establish diplomatic relations, as we would try
to do today if somehow the land and people of Italy had
just been discovered. *That's* Nordwell's point, and taken
in that way his analogy makes a good argument.

One famous argument uses an analogy to try to establish the existence of a Creator of the world. We can infer
the existence of a Creator from the order and beauty of
the world, this argument claims, just as we can infer the
existence of an architect or carpenter when we see a
beautiful and well-built house. Spelled out in premise-
and-conclusion form:

> Beautiful and well-built houses must have "makers": intelligent designers and builders.
>
> The world is *like* a beautiful and well-built house.
>
> Therefore, the world must also have a "maker": an intelligent Designer and Builder, God.

Again, more examples are not needed here; it is the similarity of the world to *one* example, a house, which the argument wishes to stress.

Whether the world really *is* relevantly similar to a house, though, is not so clear. We know quite a bit about the causes of houses. But houses are *parts* of nature. We know very little, actually, about the structure of nature as a *whole*, or about what sort of causes it might be expected to have. David Hume discusses this argument in his *Dialogues Concerning Natural Religion*, and asks:

> Is *part* of nature a rule for the whole? ... Think [of how] wide a step you have taken when you compared houses ... to the universe, and from their similarity in some circumstances inferred a similarity in their causes. ... Does not the great disproportion bar all comparison and inference?*

The world is different from a house in at least this: a house is part of a larger whole, the world, while the world itself (the universe) is the largest of wholes. Thus Hume suggests that the universe is *not* relevantly similar to a house. Houses indeed imply "Makers" beyond themselves, but—as far as we know—the universe as a whole may contain its cause within itself. This analogy, then, makes a poor argument.

Dialogues concerning Natural Religion (Indianapolis: Hackett Publishing Company, 1980), Part II.

IV

Arguments from Authority

Often we must rely on others to find out and tell us what we cannot find out on our own. We cannot test every new consumer product for ourselves, for example; we cannot know firsthand what the trial of Socrates was like; most of us cannot judge from our own experience whether prisoners in other countries are mistreated. Instead we must argue in the following general way:

> X (some person or organization who ought to know) says that Y.
>
> Therefore, Y is true.

Arguments in this form are *arguments from authority*. For instance:

> Human rights monitoring organizations say that some prisoners are mistreated in Mexico.
>
> Therefore, some prisoners are mistreated in Mexico.

Relying on others, however, is sometimes a risky business. Consumer products are not always tested fairly, historical sources have their biases, and so may human rights monitoring organizations. Once again we must consider a checklist of requirements that any good argument from authority must meet.

(13) Sources should be cited

Factual assertions not otherwise defended may be supported by reference to the appropriate sources. Some factual assertions, of course, are so obvious that they do not need support at all. It is usually not necessary to *prove* that the population of the United States is more than 200 million, or that Juliet loved Romeo. However, a more precise figure for the population of the United States or, say, for the current rate of population growth, *does* need a citation. Likewise, the claim that Juliet was only fourteen should cite a few Shakespearean lines in support.

Citation has two purposes. One is to help establish the reliability of the premise: remember rule 3. A person or organization is less likely to be misquoted if an exact reference is given: the author knows that readers can check. The other purpose of a citation is precisely to allow the reader or hearer to find the information on his or her own. Citations should therefore include all the necessary information.

NO:

Human rights monitoring organizations say that some prisoners are mistreated in Mexico.

Therefore, some prisoners are mistreated in Mexico.

YES:

Amnesty International reports in the January 1985 issue
of *Amnesty International Newsletter* (volume XV, number 1,
p. 6) that some prisoners are mistreated in Mexico. Therefore, some prisoners are mistreated in Mexico.

(14) Are the sources informed?

Sources must be *qualified* to make the statements they
make. The Census Bureau is entitled to make claims
about the population of the United States. Auto
mechanics are qualified to discuss the merits of different
automobiles, doctors are qualified on matters of medicine, ecologists and earth scientists on the environmental
effects of pollution, and so on. These sources are qualified because they have the appropriate background and
information.

Where an authority's background or information are
not immediately clear, an argument must explain them
briefly. The argument cited in section 13, for example,
must be expanded farther:

Amnesty International reports in the January 1985 issue
of *Amnesty International Newsletter* (volume XV, number 1,
p. 6) that some prisoners are mistreated in Mexico.
Amnesty International reports having heard of police ill-
treatment of suspects in the state of Sinaloa for several
years, and the article cited above reports the testimony of
one of them in detail. Jose Antonio Nunez Villareal was
tortured by the police after being arrested on ordinary criminal charges, and since his release has required two major
operations; doctors told him that he very nearly died.

An informed source need not fit our general stereo-
type of "an authority"—and a person who fits our stereo-

type of an authority may not even be an informed source.

NO:

> President Bernard of Topheavy College told parents and reporters today that classrooms at Topheavy promote lively and free exchange of ideas. Therefore, classrooms at Topheavy do indeed promote lively and free exchange of ideas.

The President of a college may know very little about what happens in its classrooms.

YES:

> An accreditation committee's tabulation of all student course evaluations for the last three years at Topheavy College shows that only 5.3% of all students answered "Yes" when asked whether classes at Topheavy promoted lively and free exchange of ideas. Therefore, classes at Topheavy seldom promote lively and free exchange of ideas.

In this case, students are the most informed sources.

Also, authorities on one subject are not necessarily informed about every subject on which they offer opinions.

> Einstein was a pacifist; therefore pacifism must be right.

Einstein's genius in physics does not establish him as a genius in political philosophy.

Sometimes, of course, we must rely on authorities whose knowledge is better than ours but still less than perfect. Countries that mistreat their prisoners, for example, usually try to hide that fact, so organizations like Amnesty International must sometimes rely on frag-

mentary information. If you must rely on an authority
with incomplete information, but still better information
than your own, acknowledge the problem. Often incomplete information is better than none at all.

Finally, beware of supposed authorities who claim to
know what they could not possibly know. If a book
claims to be "written as if the author had been a fly on
the wall of the most closely guarded room in the Pentagon,"* you know without even reading it that it is a
book full of conjecture, gossip, rumors, and other
untrustworthy information (unless, of course, the author
really *was* a fly on the wall of the most closely guarded
room in the Pentagon). Similarly, religious moralists
have often declared that certain practices are wrong
because they are contrary to the will of God. We should
respond that God ought to be spoken for a little more
cautiously. God's will is not easy to ascertain, and when
God speaks so softly it is easy to confuse His will with
our own peculiar moral prejudices.

(15) Are the sources impartial?

People who have the most at stake in a dispute are usually not the best sources of information about the issues
involved. Sometimes they may not even tell the truth.
The person accused in a criminal trial is presumed innocent until proven guilty, but we seldom completely
believe his or her claim to be innocent without some
confirmation from impartial witnesses. But even a will-
ingness to tell the truth as one sees it is not always
enough. The truth as one honestly sees it can still be
biased. We tend to see what we expect to see: we notice,

---

*Advertisement in *The New York Times Book Review*, 12/9/84,
p. 3.

remember, and pass on information that supports our point of view, but we are not quite so motivated when the evidence points the other way.

Don't rely on the President, then, if the issue is the effectiveness of the Administration's policies. Don't rely on the government for the best information on the human rights situation in countries which the government happens to support or oppose. Don't rely on interest groups on *either* side of a major public question for the most accurate information on the issues at stake. Don't rely on a product's manufacturer for the best information concerning that product.

NO:

Epson claims that its FX80 dot-matrix computer printer prints at a rate of 160 characters per second. Therefore, the Epson FX80 dot-matrix computer printer does indeed print at about 160 characters per second.

Sources should be impartial. The best information on consumer products comes from the independent consumer magazines and testing agencies, because these agencies are unaffiliated with any manufacturer and must answer consumers who want the most accurate information they can get.

YES:

Consumer Reports tested the Epson FX80 dot-matrix computer printer and found that it prints at 19 characters per second. Therefore, the Epson FX80 dot-matrix computer printer prints at about 19 characters per second.*

---

*This and the above information come from *Consumer Reports'* *1984 Buying Guide Issue*, vol. 48, number 12 (Mount Vernon, New

Independent servicepeople and mechanics are relatively impartial sources of information. Amnesty International is an impartial source on the human rights situations in other countries because it is not trying to support or oppose any specific government. On political matters, so long as the disagreements are basically over statistics, look to independent government agencies, such as the Census Bureau, or to university studies or other independent sources. For handgun statistics, for example, look to the National Center for Crime Statistics, not to the National Rifle Association.

Make sure that the source is *genuinely* independent and not just an interest group masquerading under an independent-sounding name. Check their sources of funding; check their other publications; check the tone of the report or book which is quoted. At the very least, try to confirm for yourself any factual claim quoted from a potentially biased source. Good arguments cite their sources (rule 13); look them up. Make sure that the evidence is quoted correctly and not pulled out of context, and check for further information that might be relevant. You are then entitled to cite those sources yourself.

(16) Cross-check sources

When experts disagree, you cannot rely on any of them. Before you quote any person or organization as an authority, you should check to make sure that other equally qualified and impartial people or organizations agree. One strength of Amnesty International's reports, for instance, is that they usually are corroborated by reports from other independent human rights monitor-

York: Consumers Union of the United States, December, 1983), p. 96.

ing organizations. (Again, they often *conflict* with the reports of governments, but governments are often not impartial.)

Authorities agree chiefly on specific factual questions. Whether or not a prisoner has been tortured is a specific factual issue, and it is often possible to verify. But as issues become larger and more intangible, it becomes harder to find authorities who agree. On many philosophical issues it is difficult to quote anyone as an uncontested expert. Aristotle disagreed with Plato, Hegel with Kant. You may be able to use their *arguments*, then, but no philosopher will be convinced if you merely quote another philosopher's conclusions.

(17) Personal attacks do not disqualify a source

Supposed authorities may be disqualified if they are *not* informed, impartial, or largely in agreement. *Other* sorts of attacks on authorities are not legitimate. Ludwig von Mises describes a series of illegitimate attacks on the economist Ricardo:

> In the eyes of the Marxians the Ricardian theory is spurious because Ricardo was a bourgeois. The German racists condemn the same theory because Ricardo was a Jew, and the German nationalists because he was an Englishman.... Some German professors advanced all three arguments together against the validity of Ricardo's teaching.*

This is the "ad hominem" fallacy: attacking the *person* of an authority rather than his or her qualifications.

---

*L. v. Mises, *Human Action* (New Haven: Yale University Press, 1963), p. 75.

Ricardo's class, religion, and nationality are irrelevant to the possible truth of his theories. To disqualify him as an authority, those "German professors" have to show that his evidence was incomplete– that is, they have to show that his judgments were not fully *informed*–or that he was not impartial, or that other equally reputable economists disagree with his findings. Otherwise, personal attacks only disqualify the *attacker*!

V

Arguments about Causes

We sometimes try to explain why something happens by arguing about its *cause*. Suppose, for instance, that you wonder why some of your friends are more open-minded than others. You talk to your friends and discover that most of the open-minded ones are also well-read—they keep up with newspapers, read literature, and so on —while most of the less open-minded ones are not. You discover, in other words, that there is a *correlation* between being well-read and being open-minded. Then, because being well-read seems to be correlated with open-mindedness, you might conclude that being well-read *leads* to open-mindedness.

Arguments from correlation to cause are widely used in the medical and social sciences. To find out whether eating a full breakfast improves your health, doctors do a study to find out whether people who usually eat a full breakfast live longer than people who usually don't. To find out whether reading really does tend to make a person more open-minded, a psychologist might devise a test for open-mindedness and a survey of reading habits, give the tests to a representative sample of the population, and then check to see whether a higher proportion of the regular readers are also open-minded.

Formal tests like these usually enter our arguments as arguments from authority: we rely on the authority of the people who did the tests, looking to their credentials and to their professional colleagues to make sure they are informed and impartial. We do have an obligation, however, to read and report their studies carefully, and to try to assess them as best we can.

Our own arguments about causes usually have less carefully selected examples. We may argue from some striking cases in our own experience, or from our knowledge of our friends or of history. These arguments are often speculative—but then, so are their more formal cousins done by doctors and psychologists. Sometimes it is very difficult to know what causes what. This chapter offers several questions to ask of any argument about causes, and then a set of reminders about the pitfalls of moving from correlation to cause.

(18) Does the argument explain how cause leads to effect?

When we think that A causes B, we usually believe not only that A and B are correlated but also that it "makes sense" for A to cause B. Good arguments, then, do not just appeal to the correlation of A and B: they also explain *why* it "makes sense" for A to cause B.

NO:

> Most of my open-minded friends are well-read; most of my less open-minded friends are not. Reading, then, seems to lead to open-mindedness.

YES:

> Most of my open-minded friends are well-read; most of my less open-minded friends are not. It seems likely that the more you read, the more you encounter challenging new ideas, ideas that make you less confident of your own. Reading also lifts you out of your daily world and shows you how different and many-sided life can be. Reading, then, seems to lead to open-mindedness.

This argument could be more specific, but it does fill in the important connections between cause and effect.

More formal and statistical arguments about causes —in medicine, for example—also must try to fill in the connections between the causes and the effects they postulate. Doctors don't stop with evidence that merely demonstrates that eating a full breakfast is correlated with improved health; they also want to know *why* eating a full breakfast improves health.

> Doctors N. B. Belloc and L. Breslow, respectively of the Human Population Laboratory of the California Department of Public Health and of the Department of Preventive and Social Medicine at UCLA, followed 7000 adults for five and a half years, relating life expectancy and health to certain basic health habits. They found that eating a full breakfast is correlated with greater life expectancy. (See Belloc and Breslow, "The Relation of Physical Health Status and Health Practices," *Preventive Medicine*, volume 1 (August, 1972), pp. 409–421.) It seems probable that people who eat a full breakfast get more of the necessary nutrients than people who skip breakfast or go through the morning on snacks and coffee. It is also likely that if the body starts out the day with a good meal, it metabolizes later meals more efficiently. Thus, it seems likely that eating a full breakfast leads to better health.

Notice that this argument not only explains how cause may lead to effect but also cites its source and explains why that source is an informed source.

(19) Does the conclusion propose the most likely cause?

Most events have many possible causes. Just finding a possible cause, then, is not enough: you must go on to show that it is the most *likely* cause. It is always possible that the "Bermuda Triangle" really is inhabited by supernatural beings who protect their domain from human intrusion. It's *possible*. But the supernatural explanation is highly unlikely compared to the other likely explanations for the disappearance of ships and planes: tropical storms, unpredictable wind and wave patterns, etc. (If indeed there *is* anything unusual about the Bermuda Triangle at all: remember section 10.) Only if these everyday explanations fail to account for the facts should we begin to consider alternative hypotheses.

Likewise, it is always possible that people become open-minded, or at least tolerant, because they are just tired of arguing. Maybe they just want to "let the long contention cease," as Matthew Arnold put it. It's *possible*. But we also know that not very many people are like that. Most people who have dogmatic views stick up for them; it just pains them too much to see other people going astray. Therefore, it seems more likely that people who become tolerant have truly become open-minded, and reading remains a likely cause.

How do we know which explanations are most likely? One rule of thumb is: prefer explanations which are compatible with our best-established knowledge. Natural science is well-established; so is our ordinary understanding of what people are like. Sometimes the most likely explanation may still be wrong, of course, but we have to start with our best guesses. "Well-established knowledge" is there for a reason.

Sometimes additional evidence is necessary before *any* explanation can be accepted with much confidence. More evidence is necessary when several competing "natural" explanations all fit the available evidence. Rules 20–23, though not exhaustive, explain some of the most common types of competing explanations.

(20) Correlated events are not necessarily related

Some correlations are just coincidental.

> Ten minutes after I took "Doctor Hartshorne's Insomnia Bitters," I was sound asleep. Therefore, "Doctor Hartshorne's Insomnia Bitters" put me to sleep.

Here the event being explained is my going to sleep. Because my going to sleep was correlated with my taking "Doctor Hartshorne's Insomnia Bitters," the argument concludes that taking the "Bitters" was the *cause* of my going to sleep. However, although "Doctor Hartshorne's Insomnia Bitters" *may* have put me to sleep, I may also have fallen asleep on my own. Maybe it had nothing to do with the "Bitters." Maybe I was very tired, and took the "Bitters" shortly before I would have fallen asleep anyway.

Doctor Hartshorne could have her day in court. We would need to set up a controlled experiment, with one group of people using the "Bitters" and another group not using it. If more of the people who used it fell asleep faster than the people who did not use it, then it may have some medicinal value after all. But mere correlation, by itself, does not *establish* a cause-and-effect relationship. The rise and fall of women's hemlines has correlated for years with the rise and fall of the Dow Jones

Industrial Average, but who thinks that one causes the other? The world is just full of coincidences.

(21) Correlated events may have a common cause

Some correlations are not relations between cause and effect but represent two effects of some *other* cause. It is quite possible, for instance, that being well-read and being open-minded are both caused by some third factor: by going to college, for example. Being well-read, then, might *not* itself lead to open-mindedness: instead, going to college leads to open-mindedness (maybe by exposing a person to many different points of view), and helps a person become well-read as well. You may need to survey your friends again: find out which ones went to college!

Or:

Television is ruining our morals. Shows on television portray violence, callousness, and depravity—and just look around us!

The suggestion here is that "immorality" on television causes "immorality" in real life. It is at least as likely, however, that *both* televised "immorality" *and* real-life "immorality" are caused instead by more basic common causes, such as the breakup of traditional value-systems, the absence of constructive pastimes, etc. Or again:

Over the past 20 years, children have watched more and more television. Over the same period, college admission test scores have steadily declined. Watching television seems to ruin your mind.

The suggestion is that watching television causes lower test scores. It would be useful, for a start, if this argument explained exactly how the alleged cause, watching television, leads to this effect (rule 18). In any case, other explanations seem at least as good. Maybe something quite different accounts for the drop in test scores—a drop in the quality of the schools, for example—which would suggest that the two correlated trends are not related (rule 20). Then again, possibly, *both* watching television *and* lower test scores might be caused instead by some common cause. Maybe, for instance, the lack of more challenging pastimes is again at fault.

(22) *Either of two correlated events may cause the other*

Correlation also does not establish the *direction* of causality. After all, the very same correlation that suggests that television is "ruining" our morals could equally well suggest that our morals are "ruining" television. So yet another kind of alternative hypothesis also needs evaluation.

This problem affects even the most advanced studies of correlations. Psychologists might devise a test for open-mindedness and a survey of reading habits, give the tests to a representative sample of the population, and then check to see whether an unusually high proportion of the readers are also open-minded. Suppose that there is indeed a correlation. It still does not follow that reading *leads* to open-mindedness. Open-mindedness might lead instead to reading! After all, people who are open-minded may be more likely to seek out a variety of papers and books in the first place. This is one reason that it is important to explain the connections between cause and effect. If you can fill in plausible connections from A to B but not from B to A, then it seems likely that A leads to B rather than vice versa. If B could lead to A as plausibly as A leads to B, though, then you cannot tell which direction the cause goes—or perhaps it goes both ways.

(23) Causes may be complex

It is occasionally argued that pedestrian walkways across streets are more dangerous than unmarked streets, because crosswalks seem to be correlated with a higher, not lower, number of accidents. Often the suggested conclusion is that walkways themselves cause accidents, perhaps by creating in their users a "false sense of security." Remembering rule 22, though, we should also consider the possibility that the causal connection runs the other way. Maybe, in a manner of speaking, accidents cause crosswalks. Crosswalks don't just appear arbitrarily, after all: they tend to be put at places where accidents have frequently happened. But they may not necessarily solve the problem, and even if they help they might not eliminate *all* the accidents.

Moreover, once a crosswalk is installed, still more people are likely to use it. So we might well expect the *number* of people involved in accidents at these locations to increase, rather than decrease, although the accident *rate* should decrease.

Clearly this story is a complex one. A false sense of security might well play some role, especially if the accident rate has not decreased as sharply as we might expect; at the same time we should not forget that crosswalks are usually put precisely at places where accidents tend to happen. Again, causes need not be either-or: sometimes the answer is "both."

Many causal stories are complex. Maybe, again, reading makes you more open-minded, but it is surely also true, as section 22 pointed out, that open-mindedness is likely to lead some people to read more. Maybe eating a full breakfast improves your health, but maybe healthy people are also precisely people who are inclined to eat a full breakfast in the first place. Don't overstate your conclusion, then: seldom do we fasten onto *the* one and only cause. Causal arguments are important because even finding *a* cause is often useful. Just to know that eating a full breakfast is correlated with better health, and *probably* leads to better health, may be enough of a reason to try to eat fuller breakfasts.

VI

Deductive Arguments

The arguments we have considered so far are all uncertain in one way or another. New examples might always refute an argument from example, and even an informed and impartial source might be wrong. Properly formed *deductive arguments*, however, are arguments the truth of whose premises guarantees the truth of their conclusions.

> If there are no chance factors in chess, then chess is a game of pure skill.
>
> There are no chance factors in chess.
>
> Therefore, chess is a game of pure skill.

If these two premises are true, then it *must* also be true that chess is a game of pure skill. To disagree with the conclusion, you'd also have to disagree with at least one of the premises.

Deductive arguments offer certainty, then—but only if the *premises* are also known with certainty. Since the premises of our arguments usually cannot be known with certainty, the conclusions of real-life deductive arguments still have to be taken with a few (sometimes many!) grains of salt. Still, when strong premises can be found, deductive forms are very useful. Remember rule 3: try to start with reliable premises.

Even when the premises are uncertain, deductive forms offer an effective way of *organizing* an argument, especially an argumentative essay. This chapter presents six common deductive forms with simple examples, each form in a section of its own. Chapters VII–IX will return to their use in argumentative essays.

(24) Modus Ponens

Properly formed deductive arguments are called *valid* arguments. Using the letters **p** and **q** to stand for sentences, the simplest valid deductive form is:

> If [sentence **p**] then [sentence **q**].
> [Sentence **p**].
> Therefore, [sentence **q**].

Or, more briefly:

> If **p** then **q**.
> **p**.
> Therefore, **q**.

This form is called modus ponens ("the mode of affirming"). Taking **p** to stand for "There are no chance factors in chess" and **q** to stand for "Chess is a game of pure skill," our introductory example follows modus ponens.

Often an argument in this form is so obvious that it does not need to be stated as an official modus ponens at all.

Since optimists are more likely to succeed than pessimists, you should be an optimist.

This argument could be written:

If optimists are more likely to succeed than pessimists, then you should be an optimist.

Optimists *are* more likely to succeed than pessimists.

Therefore, you should be an optimist.

but the argument is perfectly clear without putting it in this form. At other times, however, writing out the modus ponens is useful:

If there are millions of habitable planets in our galaxy, then it seems likely that life has evolved on more than just this one.

There are millions of habitable planets in our galaxy.

Therefore, it seems likely that life has evolved on more than just this one.

To develop this argument you must explain and defend both of its premises, and they require quite different arguments (why?). It is useful, then, to state them clearly and separately from the start.

(25) Modus Tollens

A second valid form is modus tollens ("the mode of denying"):

If **p** then **q**.

Not-**q**.

Therefore, not-**p**.

Here "Not-**q**" simply stands for the denial of **q**, i.e., for the sentence "It is not true that **q**"; similarly for "not-**p**."

Remember Sherlock Holmes's argument, which we discussed in section 1:

A dog was kept in the stalls, and yet, though someone had been in and fetched out a horse, he had not barked . . . Obviously the visitor was someone whom the dog knew well . . .

Holmes's argument is a modus tollens:

If the dog did not know the visitor well, then the dog would have barked.

The dog did not bark.

Therefore, the dog knew the visitor well.

To write this argument in symbols, use **k** for "The dog did not know the visitor well" and **b** for "The dog barked."

If **k** then **b**.

Not-**b**.

Therefore, not-**k**.

"Not-**b**" stands for "The dog did not bark," and "not-**k**" stands for "It is not true that the dog did not know the visitor well," i.e., "The dog *did* know the visitor well."*

---

*We might instead have defined **k** as "The dog did know the visitor well," so that in symbols the argument goes:

Astronomer Fred Hoyle wields an interesting modus tollens. To paraphrase a bit:

> If the universe were infinitely old, there would be no hydrogen left in it, since hydrogen is steadily converted into helium throughout the universe, and this conversion is a one-way process. But in fact the universe consists almost entirely of hydrogen. Thus the universe must have had a definite beginning.

To put Hoyle's argument in symbols, use **i** to stand for "The universe is infinitely old" and **h** to stand for "No hydrogen is left in the universe."

If **i** then **h**.

Not-**h**.

Therefore, not-**i**.

"Not-**h**" stands for "It is not true that there is no hydrogen left in the universe" (or: "The universe does contain hydrogen"); "not-**i**" means "It is not true that the universe is infinitely old." Hoyle goes on to rephrase the conclusion: because the universe is not infinitely old, there must have been a definite point at which it began.

If not-**k** then **b**.

Not-**b**.

Therefore, **k**.

Strictly speaking, the conclusion then is "Not-not-**k**"–"It is not true that it is not true that the dog knew the visitor well"– but this is logically equivalent simply to **k**.

(26) Hypothetical Syllogism

A third valid form is hypothetical syllogism:

> If **p** then **q**.
> If **q** then **r**.
> Therefore, if **p** then **r**.

For instance:

> If you **s**tudy other cultures, then you **r**ealize what a variety of human customs there is.
>
> If you **r**ealize what a variety of human customs there is, then you **q**uestion your own customs.
>
> Therefore, if you **s**tudy other cultures, then you **q**uestion your own customs.

Using the letters in boldface to stand for the component sentences in this statement, we have:

> If **s** then **r**.
> If **r** then **q**.
> Therefore, if **s** then **q**.

Hypothetical syllogism is valid for any number of premises as long as each premise has the form "If **p** then **q**" and the **q** of one premise becomes the **p** of the next. In section 5, for example, we considered an argument with the two premises above but also a third:

> If you **q**uestion your own customs, then you become more **t**olerant.

From this and the two premises above you can validly conclude "If **s** then **t**" by hypothetical syllogism.

Notice that hypothetical syllogism offers a good model for explaining the connections between cause and effect (rule 18). The conclusion links a cause and an effect; the premises explain the stages in between.

(27) Disjunctive Syllogism

A fourth valid form is disjunctive syllogism:

> **p** or **q**.
>
> Not-**p**.
>
> Therefore, **q**.

Consider, for instance, Bertrand Russell's argument discussed in section 2:

> Either we hope for progress through improving **m**orals, or we hope for progress through improving **i**ntelligence.
>
> We can't hope for progress through improving **m**orals.
>
> Therefore, we must hope for progress through improving **i**ntelligence.

Again using the boldface letters as symbols, this argument goes:

> **m** or **i**.
>
> Not-**m**.
>
> Therefore, **i**.

In English the word "or" can have two different meanings. In its "exclusive" sense, the word "or" in the sentence "**a** or **b**" means that either **a** or **b** is true, but not both. In its "inclusive" sense "**a** or **b**" means that either **a** or **b** is true, and possibly both. Disjunctive syllogisms are valid regardless of which sense of "or" is used, but *only in the exclusive sense of "or"* is it valid to argue:

> **p** or **q**.
> **p**.
> Therefore, not-**q**.

Suppose, for example, that someone argues:

> Only Zbignew or Zoltan could have done the dreadful deed. Zoltan did it; therefore Zbignew did not.

Zbignew's innocence depends on what the word "or" means in the first sentence. If the dreadful deed was something that only one person could have done, then the "or" is exclusive and the argument is valid. If the dreadful deed could have been a joint production, however, then the "or" remains inclusive, and Zoltan's guilt does not prove Zbignew's innocence.

(28) Dilemma

A fifth valid form is the dilemma.

> **p** or **q**.
> If **p** then **r**.
> If **q** then **s**.
> Therefore, **r** or **s**.

Arguments in dilemma form are common in political debates. Opponents of a new weapons system, for example, might argue in this way:

> Either the new system will work or it will not work.
>
> If it works, it will force the other side to build similar weapons in response, leaving the balance of power unchanged.
>
> If it does not work, then it will be a huge waste of money.
>
> Therefore, building the new system will either leave the balance of power unchanged, or it will be a huge waste of money.

In symbols:

> w or not-w.
> If w then u.
> If not-w then m.
> Therefore, u or m.

The point of this argument, of course, is that the new system should not be built at all. If necessary, you might spell it out with another argument in dilemma form, beginning with the conclusion of the last one:

> Building the new system will either leave the balance of power unchanged, or it will be a huge waste of money.
>
> If building the new system will leave the balance of power unchanged, we should not build it.
>
> If building the new system will be a huge waste of money, then we should not build it.

Therefore, we should not build the new system.

In symbols:

u or **m**.
If **u** then not-**b**.
If **m** then not-**b**.
Therefore, not-**b**.

Technically the conclusion is "Not-**b** or not-**b**," but this statement is equivalent simply to "Not-**b**."

(29) *Reductio ad Absurdum*

One traditional deductive strategy deserves special mention even though, strictly speaking, it is only a version of modus tollens. This is the reductio ad absurdum, i.e., a "reduction to absurdity."

To prove: **p**.
Assume: Not-**p** (that is, that **p** is false).
From the assumption derive an implication: **q**.
Show: **q** is false (contradictory, silly, "absurd").
Conclude: **p**.

Arguments by "reductio," as these arguments are often called, thus establish their conclusions by showing that the denial of the conclusion leads to absurdity. There is nothing left to do, the argument suggests, but to accept the conclusion.

Remember, for example, the argument for the existence of a Creator which we discussed in section 12. Houses have creators, the argument goes, and the world is *like* a house—it too is ordered and beautiful. Thus, the analogy suggests, the world must have a Creator too. Section 12 quoted David Hume to the effect that the world is not relevantly enough similar to a house for this analogy to succeed. In Part V of his *Dialogues* Hume also suggests a reductio ad absurdum of the analogy. Paraphrasing:

> It seems clear that the world is not wholly perfect. Now when houses are not perfect, we know who to blame: the carpenters and masons are not perfect either. If we must reason by analogy, then, it seems to follow from the imperfections of the *world* that *God* is not perfect. But you would consider this conclusion absurd. Since this absurd result follows from your own analogy, however, the only way to avoid the absurdity is to reject the analogy itself. Therefore, God cannot be known by analogy!

Spelled out in reductio form, we have:

> *To prove*: God cannot be known by analogy.
>
> *Assume*: God *can* be known by analogy.
>
> *From the assumption it follows that*: God is imperfect (because the *world* is imperfect).
>
> *But*: God cannot be imperfect.
>
> *Therefore*: God cannot be known by analogy.*

Not everyone would find the idea of an imperfect God "absurd," of course, but Hume knew that the Christians with whom he was arguing would not accept it.

———————————

*For practice, translate this argument as a modus tollens.

(30) Deductive arguments in several steps

Many valid forms are *combinations* of the simple forms introduced in sections 24–29. Here, for example, is Sherlock Holmes performing a simple deduction for Doctor Watson's edification, meanwhile commenting on the relative roles of observation and deduction. Holmes has casually remarked that Watson has been to a certain Post Office that morning, and furthermore that he sent off a telegram while there. "Right!" replies Watson, amazed, "right on both points! But I confess that I don't see how you arrived at it." Holmes:

> "It is simplicity itself ... Observation tells me that you have a little reddish mold adhering to your instep. Just opposite the Wigmore Street Post Office they have taken up the pavement and thrown up some earth, which lies in such a way that it is difficult to avoid treading in it in entering. The earth is of this peculiar reddish tint which is found, as far as I know, nowhere else in the neighborhood. So much is observation. The rest is deduction."
>
> [Watson]: "How, then, did you deduce the telegram?"
>
> [Holmes]: "Why, of course I knew that you had not written a letter, since I sat opposite you all morning. I see also in your open desk there that you have a sheet of stamps and a thick bundle of postcards. What could you go to the Post Office for, then, but to send a wire? Eliminate all the other factors, and the one which remains must be the truth."*

Putting Holmes's deduction into more explicit premises, we might have:

1. Watson has a little reddish mold on his boots.

---

*A. Conan Doyle, *The Sign of the Four*, Chapter I.

2. If Watson has a little reddish mold on his boots, then he has been to the Wigmore Street Post Office this morning (because there and only there is reddish dirt of that sort thrown up, and in a way difficult to avoid stepping in).

3. If Watson has been to the Wigmore Street Post Office this morning, he either mailed a letter, bought stamps or cards, or sent a wire.

4. If Watson had gone to the Post Office to mail a letter, he would have written the letter this morning.

5. Watson wrote no letter this morning.

6. If Watson had gone to the Post Office to buy stamps or cards, he would not already have a drawer full of stamps and cards.

7. Watson already has a drawer full of stamps and cards.

8. Therefore, Watson sent a wire at the Wigmore Street Post Office this morning.

We now need to break the argument down into a series of valid arguments in the simple forms presented in sections 24–29. We might start with a hypothetical syllogism:

2. If Watson has a little reddish mold on his boots, then he has been to the Wigmore Street Post Office this morning.

3. If Watson has been to the Wigmore Street Post Office this morning, he either mailed a letter, bought stamps or cards, or sent a wire.

A. Therefore, if Watson has a little reddish mold on his boots, he either mailed a letter, bought stamps or cards, or sent a wire at the Wigmore Street Post Office this morning.

(I will use "A," "B," etc. to stand for the conclusions of simple arguments, which can then be used as premises to draw further conclusions.) Now with A and 1 we can use modus ponens:

A. If Watson has a little reddish mold on his boots, he either mailed a letter, bought stamps or cards, or sent a wire at the Wigmore Street Post Office this morning.
1. Watson has a little reddish mold on his boots.
B. Therefore, Watson either mailed a letter, bought stamps or cards, or sent a wire at the Wigmore Street Post Office this morning.

Two of these three possibilities can now be ruled out, both by modus tollens.

4. If Watson had gone to the Post Office to mail a letter, he would have written the letter this morning.
5. Watson wrote no letter this morning.
C. Therefore, Watson did not go to the Post Office to mail a letter.

and:

6. If Watson had gone to the Post Office to buy stamps or cards, he would not already have a drawer full of stamps and cards.
7. Watson already has a drawer full of stamps and cards.
D. Therefore, Watson did not go to the Post Office to buy stamps or cards.

Finally, then:

B. Watson either mailed a letter, bought stamps or cards, or sent a wire at the Wigmore Street Post Office this morning.
C. Watson did not go to the Post Office to mail a letter.
D. Watson did not go to the Post Office to buy stamps or cards.
8. Therefore, Watson sent a wire at the Wigmore Street Post Office this morning.

This last inference is an extended disjunctive syllogism. "Eliminate all the other factors, and the one which remains must be the truth."

VII

Composing an Argumentative Essay

A. Exploring the Issue

We now move from writing short arguments to writing longer ones: from arguments in paragraphs to arguments in essays. An argumentative essay is often an elaboration of a short argument, or a series of short arguments held together by a larger design. But the process of thinking and "designing" an argumentative essay makes it much different from a short argument.

The next three chapters correspond to the three stages of writing an argumentative essay. Chapter VII is about *Exploring the Issue*, Chapter VIII sets out the *Main Points of the Argumentative Essay*, and Chapter IX is about actually *Writing the Essay*. The rules in these chapters are prefixed by an *A, B,* or *C*.

The Introduction distinguished two main uses of arguments: to *inquire* into the merits of a position, and to *defend* a position once your inquiry has led to fruits. The first step is inquiry. Before you can write an argumentative essay you must explore the issue and think through the various positions for yourself.

(A1) Explore the arguments on all sides of the issue

Some people have recently proposed a "voucher plan" for elementary and secondary schools. Under this plan, the tax money that currently goes to the public school system would be divided equally among children's parents in the form of "vouchers" which they could transfer to the school of their choice, including private and parochial schools. The government would regulate competing schools to make sure that they all met minimal standards, but people would be free to choose whatever school they wished as long as it met those standards.

Suppose you are assigned the voucher plan as a topic for an argumentative essay. Do *not* begin by pulling up the typewriter and writing out some argument for the opinion that first occurs to you. You are not being asked for the opinion that first occurs to you. You are being asked to *arrive at* a well-informed opinion which can be defended with solid arguments. It takes some time.

First, find out what each side considers the strongest arguments for its position. Read articles or talk to people with *different* viewpoints.

The strongest argument for the pro-voucher side is probably "freedom of choice." The voucher plan, it is claimed, would lead to a much wider range of alternative schools than now exist, and it would not penalize parents for choosing one of them over another (as the present system does, since everyone must pay taxes to support the public schools even if their children do not attend). The main argument *against* vouchers seems to be that the public schools mirror the real world: we have to learn to live with and appreciate people who are *not* like us and with whom we might *not* choose to go to school if we had the choice. Public schools, it is claimed, make democratic citizens.

As you examine the issue you will find arguments for and against these claims. You will also begin to formulate arguments of your own. Assess these arguments using the rules in Chapters I–VI. Try out different argument forms, make as good an argument as you can for each side, and then criticize these arguments using our rules.

Consider arguments by *analogy*. Have we tried anything *like* the voucher system before? Perhaps: competing colleges and universities, though not paid for by vouchers, seem to offer a variety of good educations, which suggests that a system of competing primary and secondary schools might have similar results. But be sure that this is a relevantly similar example. At present, for example, many colleges and universities are tax-supported. Would a system without tax-supported public institutions offer good educations to as many people? Would it bring as many diverse people into contact?

Maybe there are more relevant similarities between schools under the voucher plan and the present parochial and private schools. Here you also need some arguments from *examples* and/or from *authority*. How good are the present private and parochial schools compared to the public school system? Do they produce people who are as tolerant of other people? (How good is the record of private schools on racial desegregation, for instance?)

Deductive arguments may also be useful. Here is a hypothetical syllogism:

If we set up a voucher plan, then schools would be competing for students.

If schools are competing for students, then they will use advertisements and promotions to encourage parents to "shop around."

If parents are encouraged to "shop around," then many parents will move their children from school to school.

If many parents move their children from school to school, many children will not form lasting friendships or feel secure about their surroundings.

Therefore, if we set up a voucher plan, many children will not form lasting friendships or feel secure about their surroundings.

As section 26 pointed out, hypothetical syllogisms can often be used, on both sides of an issue, to explain the connections between causes and effects. They may also be used to *work out* what those connections might be in cases where you are not sure whether there *is* a connection.

(A2) Question and defend each argument's premises

When the premises of an argument are open to question, you must consider arguments for *them* as well.

Suppose you are considering the hypothetical syllogism just sketched. You know that it is a valid argument; the conclusion does indeed follow from the premises. But you still need to be convinced that the premises are *true*. To continue exploring the issue, then, you must go another step: you must try to come up with arguments for any of the premises of the argument which might reasonably be questioned.

For example, an argument for the second premise ("If schools are competing for students, then they will use advertisements and promotions to encourage parents to 'shop around'") might use an analogy:

> When stores compete for customers, they try to offer special deals and services to make themselves look more attractive than the competition, and they advertise heavily in order draw new customers in and old customers back. Then the other stores respond with *their* special deals and *their* advertisements. Customers are drawn from store to store and then back again: they believe that they can get the best deal by "shopping around." It would be just the same with competing schools. Each school would advertise and offer special deals, and the other schools would respond. Parents would "shop around" just like grocery shoppers or department store customers do now.

Not every claim needs much defense. The first premise of the hypothetical syllogism ("If we set up a voucher plan, then schools will be competing for children") is obvious enough to assert without much argument: this is the whole *idea* of the voucher plan. The second premise did need an argument, however, and so would the fourth ("If many parents move their children from school to school, many children will not form lasting friendships or feel secure about their surroundings"). You might also have to defend some of the premises of *these* arguments in turn. In the argument for the second premise suggested above, you might go on to offer examples to show that stores do indeed offer special deals and advertise heavily in the face of heavy competition.

The rule is: any claim liable to reasonable question needs at least some defense. Naturally, space will often limit what you can say. Given limited space or time, argue chiefly for your most important and/or most controversial claims. Even then, however, cite at least *some* evidence or authority for any other claims which remain debatable.

(A3) Revise and rethink arguments as they emerge

Rules A1 and A2 outline a *process*. You may have to try several different conclusions—even opposite conclusions —before you find a view that can be defended with strong arguments. Even after you have settled on the conclusion you want to defend, you may have to try several forms before you find one that works well. Quite probably your initial argument will have to be improved. Many of the sections in Chapters I–VI illustrate how short arguments must be improved and expanded: by adding examples to an argument by example (section 8), by citing and explaining the qualifications of an authority (sections 13 and 14), and so on. Sometimes you will not be able to find enough examples, and so you may have to change your approach (or change your mind!). Sometimes you may go in search of an authority to support a claim you want to make, only to find that most authorities take the opposite view (you probably have to change your mind), or that the most informed people still disagree sharply with each other (and then you cannot argue from authority at all: remember rule 16).

Take your time. (And give yourself time to take!) This is the stage where revision is easy and experiments are cheap; indeed for some writers it is the most satisfying and creative part of writing. Use it well.

VIII

Composing an Argumentative Essay

B.   Main Points of the Essay

Suppose that you have arrived at a conclusion which you think you can defend adequately. Now you need to *organize* your essay so that it covers everything that needs to be covered, and so that you can present your argument most effectively. Get out a large sheet of scratch paper and a pencil: you are about to prepare your outline.

(B1) Explain the question

Begin by stating the question you are answering. Then explain it. Why is it important? What depends on the answer? If you are making a proposal for future actions or policies, like the voucher plan, begin by showing that

we presently have a *problem*. Why should others share
your worries or be interested in your ideas for change?
What led *you* to be concerned?

Consider your audience. If you are writing for a news-
paper or public presentation, your audience may be unaware of the issue, or unaware of the extent of the problem; your job is to make them aware. Restating the
problem can be useful even when it is no news; it helps
to locate your proposal—what problem are you trying to
solve?—and it may help remind those who are aware of
the problem but who may not have considered its importance. (If you are writing an academic essay, however,
do not try to restate the whole history of the issue. Find
out how much background your instructor expects.)

To justify your concern with a particular question or
issue, you may need to appeal to shared values and standards. Sometimes these standards are simple and uncontroversial. If you have a proposal about traffic safety,
you will probably find that its goals are obvious and
noncontroversial. Nobody likes traffic accidents. Other
arguments can appeal to standards shared by a specific
group, such as professional codes of ethics, or to institu-
tional standards, such as the standards of student con-
duct that a school endorses. They can appeal to the Constitution and to our shared political ideals, like freedom
and fairness. They can appeal to our shared ethical values, such as the sanctity of life and the importance of
individual autonomy and growth, and to broad social
values such as beauty and intellectual curiosity.

(B2) Make a definite claim or proposal

If you are making a proposal, be specific. "Something
should be done" is not a real proposal. You need not be
elaborate. "Everyone should eat breakfast" is a specific
proposal, but also a simple one. On the other hand, if

you want to argue that the United States should institute a voucher plan, some elaboration is necessary, to explain the basic idea, how payments would work, etc. Similarly, if you are making a philosophical claim, or defending your interpretation of a text or event, first state your claim or interpretation *simply* ("God exists"; "The American Civil War was caused primarily by economic conflicts," etc.); elaborate later as necessary.

If your aim is simply to assess some of the arguments for or against a claim or proposal, you may not be making a proposal of your own, or even arriving at a specific decision. For example, you may only be able to examine one line of argument in a controversy. If so, make it clear immediately that this is what you are doing. Sometimes your conclusion may simply be that the arguments for or against some position or proposal are inconclusive. Fine! But make that conclusion clear immediately. Begin by saying: "In this essay I will argue that the arguments for X are inconclusive." Otherwise, it is *your essay* that will seem inconclusive!

(B3) Develop your arguments fully

Once you are clear about the importance of the issue you are addressing, and once you have decided exactly what you intend to do in your paper, you are ready to develop your main argument.

Planning is important. Your paper has limits: don't fence more land than you can plow. One argument well-developed is better than three only sketched. Do *not* use every argument you can think of for your position: this is like preferring ten very leaky buckets to one well-sealed one. (Also, the different arguments may not always be compatible!) Concentrate on your one or two best.

If you are making a proposal, you need to show that it will solve the problem with which you began. Sometimes just stating the proposal is enough. If the problem is that your health is suffering because you do not eat a full breakfast, then eating a full breakfast is the obvious solution. If your proposal is that the United States set up a voucher plan, however, then some careful argument is necessary. You need to show that a voucher system really would encourage freedom of choice, that there would be a variety of schools available, and that these schools would be a clear improvement over the present schools. You will have to argue about cause and effect, argue from example, and so forth, and the rules discussed in previous chapters apply: use the arguments you began to develop in Chapter VII.

If you are arguing for a philosophical claim, this is the place to develop your main reason(s). If you are arguing for your interpretation of a text or event, this is the place to explain the details of that text or event and to work out your interpretation in detail. If your essay is an assessment of some of the arguments in a controversy, explain those arguments and the reasons for your assessment. Once again, remember the rules from previous chapters. If you rest a claim on an argument by example, be sure you have enough examples, representative examples, etc.; if you use a deductive form, make sure it is valid and that any questionable premises are defended as well.

(B4) Consider objections

Anticipate skeptical questions. Is your proposal affordable? Will it take too long? Has it been tried before? Can you get people to carry it out? If your proposal will be a difficult one to carry out, admit it; argue that it is worth carrying out all the same.

Most proposals have many effects, not just one. You need to consider what *dis*advantages your proposal might have. Anticipate disadvantages that others might raise as objections; bring them up yourself and respond to them. Argue that the advantages outweigh the disadvantages (and be sure, once you've considered them, that they really do!). True, the voucher plan might make schools less stable, but that might seem a small price to pay to make schools more responsive to the wishes of parents and communities. You can also argue that some possible disadvantages will not actually materialize. Maybe the schools will *not* become unstable: after all (use an argument by analogy), businesses are not destabilized when they are forced to respond to changing customer preferences.

Anticipate objections to your claim or interpretation. If you are writing an academic paper, look for criticisms of your claim or interpretation in the class readings. Once you have explored the issue carefully, you will also find objections by talking to people with different views, and in your background reading. Sift through these objections, pick the strongest and most common ones, and try to answer them.

(B5) Consider alternatives

This is an obvious rule, but it is constantly violated. If you are defending a proposal, it is not enough to show that your proposal will solve a problem. You must also show that it is *better* than other plausible ways of solving that problem under the circumstances.

> The U of Q's computer facilities are overcrowded, especially near the ends of the terms. Therefore, the U of Q should expand its computer facilities.

This argument is weak in several ways: "over-crowded" is vague, and so is the proposal. But remedying these weaknesses will not justify the conclusion. There may be other and more reasonable ways of ending the crowding. Perhaps computer time should be rationed, so that people use it more consistently instead of putting everything off until the end of the term. Or perhaps the U of Q should prohibit certain uses of the computer near the end of the term. Or perhaps the University should do nothing at all; let users readjust their use for themselves. If you still want to propose that the U of Q should expand its computer facilities, you must show that your proposal is better than any of these alternatives.

Similarly, if you are interpreting a text or event, you need to consider alternative interpretations. No matter how cleverly and thoroughly you may explain why something happened, some other explanation may seem more likely. You need to show that other explanations are *less* likely: remember rule 19. Even philosophical claims have alternatives. Does the argument from creation (section 12) show that *God* exists, or only that a *Creator* exists who might not necessarily be everything we think of when we speak of "God"? Argument is hard work!

Composing an Argumentative Essay

C. Writing

You now have explored your issue and worked out an outline. You are finally ready to write the essay itself. Remember again that writing is the *last* stage! If you have just picked up this book and opened it to this chapter, reflect: there is a reason that this is the last chapter and not the first. As the proverbial old Irishman said when a tourist asked him how to get to Dublin: if you want to get to Dublin, don't start here.

Remember too that the rules of Chapters I–VI apply to writing an essay as well as to writing short arguments. Review the rules in Chapter I in particular. Use definite, specific, concrete language; play fair; and so forth. What follow are a some additional rules specific to writing argumentative essays.

(C1) *Follow your outline*

In the last chapter you developed a five-point outline of
your argumentative essay. Follow your outline as you
begin to write. Don't wander from one point to a related
point which is supposed to come later. If you find as you
write that the essay fits together awkwardly, stop and
revise your outline; then follow the new one.

(C2) *Keep the introduction brief*

Some students use the entire first page of a four-page
argumentative essay simply to introduce the paper, often
in very general and irrelevant ways.

NO:

> Philosophers for centuries have debated about the exis-
> tence of God . . .

This is padding. It's no news to your philosophy instructor, and even someone who knew nothing at all about
the debate could write it. Get to the point.

YES:

> In this essay I will argue that God exists.

or

> This paper will argue that instituting a voucher system
> for primary and secondary education would lead to a soci-
> ety of greater intolerance and isolation between people of
> different classes.

(C3) Give your arguments one at a time

As a general rule, make one point per paragraph. Including several different points in the same paragraph only confuses the reader and lets important points slip by.

Use your main argument to plan your paragraphs. Suppose that you intend to argue against the voucher system on the grounds that under a voucher system children would not form lasting friendships or feel secure about their surroundings. First make your intentions clear (rule B2). Then you might use the hypothetical syllogism we have already sketched:

> If we set up a voucher plan, then schools would be competing for students.
>
> If schools are competing for students, then they will use advertisements and promotions to encourage parents to "shop around."
>
> If parents are encouraged to "shop around," then many parents will move their children from school to school.
>
> If many parents move their children from school to school, many children will not form lasting friendships or feel secure about their surroundings.
>
> Therefore, if we set up a voucher plan, many children will not form lasting friendships or feel secure about their surroundings.

State this argument first in an paragraph beginning "My main argument will be that ...."; you might not want to include all the steps, but give the reader a clear idea of where you are going. Then, to explain and defend this argument, devote one paragraph to each premise. The first paragraph might be brief, as the first premise does not require much defense; just explain that this is the idea of the voucher plan. The second paragraph might be the short argument for the second premise which section A2 suggested.

Follow this pattern for all arguments, not just deductions. Remember this argument from section 8:

> The right of women to vote was won only after a struggle.
>
> The right of women to attend colleges and universities was won only after a struggle.
>
> The right of women to equal employment opportunity is being won only with a struggle.
>
> The Equal Rights Amendment will be passed, if at all, only after a struggle.
>
> Therefore, all women's rights are won only after struggles.

Once again, a good essay will first explain the importance of the issue, then make the conclusion plain, and then devote a paragraph (sometimes several paragraphs) to each premise. A paragraph should defend the first premise by explaining how women won the right to vote, another several paragraphs should defend the second premise by showing with examples what a struggle it was for women to begin attending colleges and universities, and so on.

Notice, in both of these arguments, the importance of using consistent terms (rule 6). Even the short arguments considered in rule 6 were hard to understand without consistent terms, but when premises such as these become the lead sentences in separate paragraphs, it is precisely that parallel phrasing which holds the argument as a whole together.

(C4) Clarify, clarify, clarify

Maybe you know exactly what you mean; everything is clear to you. Often it is far from clear to anyone else. Points that seem connected to you may seem completely unrelated to someone reading your essay. Thus it is essential to explain the connections between your ideas, even if they seem perfectly clear to you. *How* do your premises relate to each other and support your conclusion?

NO:

> Having a choice of many schools is better than having just one. This is a traditional American value. Thus, we should set up a voucher system.

What is the connection between having many schools and "a traditional American value"? At first glance, in fact, the writer's claim seems to be false: traditionally America has favored the single public school. More carefully explained, however, there is an important idea here.

YES:

> Having a choice of many schools is better than having just one. Americans have always valued having choices: we want to have a choice among different cars or foods, among different candidates for office, among different churches. The voucher system only extends this principle to schools. Thus, we should set up a voucher system.

Clarity is important for yourself as well as for your readers. Points that *seem* connected to you may not *really* be connected, and by trying to make the connections clear you will discover that what seemed so clear to you is not really clear at all. Many times students will hand in an essay which they think is sharp and clear, only to find when they get it back that they can barely understand what they themselves were thinking when they wrote it! One good test of clarity is to put your first draft aside for a day or two and then read it again: what seemed clear late on Monday night may not make much sense Thursday morning. Another good test is to give your essay to a friend to read. Encourage him or her to be critical!

You may also have to explain your use of certain key terms. You may need to give common terms a meaning more precise than usual for purposes of your essay. This is fine as long as you *explain* your new definition, and (of course) stick to it.

(C5) Support objections with arguments

Naturally you want to develop your own arguments carefully and fully, but you also need to develop possible arguments on the *other* sides carefully and in detail, if not quite as fully as your own. Suppose, for example, that you are defending a voucher plan. When you turn to objections (rule B4) and alternatives (B5), consider how people would argue against your plan.

NO:

> Someone might object that the voucher system is unfair to poor or handicapped people. But *I* think that . . .

Why would someone object that the voucher system is unfair? What *argument* (as opposed to simple *opinion*) are you responding to?

YES:

Someone might object that the voucher system is unfair to poor or handicapped people. Handicapped students usually require more school resources than non-handicapped children, for instance, but with a voucher system their parents would receive only the same voucher as everyone else. Parents might not be able to make up the difference, and the child would be poorly provided for.

The objection about poor families, as I understand it, is this: poor families might be able to send their children only to low-budget schools which didn't charge anything above and beyond the voucher, while the rich could afford better and more varied schools. Therefore, it might be objected that the voucher system represents "freedom of choice" only for the rich.

I would respond to these objections as follows. ...

Now it is clear exactly what the objections are, and you can respond to them effectively. You might, for instance, propose special vouchers for handicapped students. You might not even have thought of this possibility if you had not detailed the arguments behind the objection, however, and your readers certainly would not have understood the point of special vouchers even if you had mentioned them.

(C6) *Don't claim more than you have shown*

End without prejudice.

NO:

In conclusion, every reason seems to favor the voucher plan, and none of the objections stands up at all. Obviously, the United States should adopt a voucher plan as quickly as possible.

YES:

I have argued in this essay that there is at least one good reason to adopt the voucher plan. Although there are some serious objections, it seems possible to modify the voucher system to deal with them. It's worth a try.

Maybe the second version overdoes it in the other direction, but you see the point. Very seldom will you answer all the objections adequately, and even when you do, new problems may surface tomorrow. "It's worth a try" is the best attitude.

X

Fallacies

Fallacies are mistakes, errors in arguments. Many of them are so tempting, and therefore so common, that they even have their own names. This may make them seem like a separate and new topic. Actually, however, to call something a fallacy is usually only another way of saying that it violates one of the rules for *good* arguments. The fallacy of "false cause," for example, is simply a questionable conclusion about cause and effect, and you can look to Chapter V for explanation.

To understand fallacies, then, you mainly need to understand what rules they break. This chapter begins by explaining two very general fallacies, referring them back to a number of rules in this book. Following that is a glossary and explanation of a number of specific fallacies, including their Latin names when frequently used.

Two General Fallacies: A Summary

(1) One of our most common errors is to draw conclusions from too little evidence. If the first Lithuanian I meet has a fiery temper, I expect that *all* Lithuanians have fiery tempers. If one ship disappears in the Bermuda Triangle, the *National Enquirer* concludes that the

Bermuda Triangle is haunted. This is the fallacy of *generalizing from incomplete information*.

It is easy to see this error when others make it, harder to see it when we do it ourselves. But consider how many of the rules in Chapters II–VI are directed against this mistake. Rule 8 requires more than one example: you cannot draw a conclusion about the entire student body of your college based on yourself and your roommate. Rule 9 requires representative examples: you cannot draw a conclusion about the entire student body of a college based on your student friends, even if you have a lot of them. Rule 10 requires background information: if you draw a conclusion about the student body of your college based on a sample of 30 people, you must also consider how big the student body is (30? 30,000?). Arguments from authority require that the *authority* not overgeneralize: he or she must have the information and the qualifications to justify the judgment you quote. Rule 19 points out that *a* cause is not necessarily *the* cause of an event. Don't overgeneralize from the fact that you have found *a* cause: other causes may be more likely.

(2) A second common fallacy is *overlooking alternatives*.

Sections 20–23 pointed out that just because events A and B are correlated, it does not follow that A causes B. B could cause A; something else could cause *both* A and B; A may cause B *and* B may cause A; or A and B might not even be related. These are all alternative explanations which you may overlook if you accept the first explanation that occurs to you. Don't rush; there are usually many more alternative explanations than you think.

> A good way to avoid divorce is to make love frequently, because figures show that spouses who make love frequently seldom seek divorce.

Here making love frequently is correlated with staying married, and is therefore supposed to be the *cause* (or *a* cause) of staying married. But staying married may also lead to couples making love frequently; something else (love and attraction!) may cause both making love frequently and staying married; each may cause the other; or possibly making love and staying married are not even related!

We also often overlook alternatives when we are trying to make decisions. Two or three options stand out, and we weigh only these. In his famous essay "Existentialism Is a Humanism," philosopher Jean-Paul Sartre tells of a student of his, during the Nazi occupation of France in World War II, who had to choose between making a risky voyage to England to fight with the Free French and staying with his mother in Paris to look after her. Sartre paints the picture as if the young man must either stake everything on a flight to England and thus totally abandon his mother, or else commit himself entirely to her and give up any hope of fighting the Nazis. But surely there are other possibilities. He could stay with his mother and still work for the Free French in Paris; he could stay with his mother for a year and try to ensure her position, gradually making it possible to leave. And are we to think of his mother as completely dependent and graspingly selfish or is she perhaps a little patriotic and possibly self-sufficient too? Very likely, then, there are other options.

On ethical issues too we tend to think in blacks and whites: either the fetus is a human being with all the rights that you and I have, or else it is a lump of tissue with no moral significance at all; either every use of animal products is wrong, or all of the current uses are

acceptable; and so on. Again, surely there are other possibilities. Try to increase the number of options you consider, not narrow them!

Glossary of the Fallacies

ad hominem: attacking the *person* of an alleged authority rather than his or her qualifications. See rule 17.

ad ignorantiam (appeal to ignorance): arguing that a claim is true just because it has not been shown to be false. A classic example is this statement by Senator Joseph McCarthy, when asked for evidence to back up his accusation that a certain person was a communist:

> I do not have much information on this except the general statement of the agency that there is nothing in the files to disprove his Communist connections.

This is an extreme example of "arguing" from *incomplete information*: here there is simply no information at all.

ad misericordiam (appeal to pity): appealing to pity as an argument for special treatment.

> I know that I flunked every exam, but if I don't pass this course, I'll have to retake it in summer school. You *have* to let me pass!

ad populum: appealing to the emotions of a crowd. Also, appealing to a person to "go along" with the crowd. E.g.: "Everyone's doing it!" **Ad populum** is a good example of a *bad* argument from authority: no reasons are offered to show that "everybody" is an informed or impartial source.

affirming the consequent: a deductive fallacy of the form:

> If **p** then **q**.
>
> **q**
>
> Therefore, **p**.

For example:

> If the roads are icy, the mail is late.
>
> The mail is late.
>
> Therefore, the roads are icy.

Both premises could be true and the conclusion still false. Although the mail *would* be late if the roads were icy, it may also be late for other reasons. The argument *overlooks alternative explanations*. Notice that this fallacy resembles modus ponens; take care!

begging the question: implicitly using your conclusion as a premise.

> God exists because it says so in the Bible, which I know
> is true because God wrote it, after all!

To write this argument in premise-and-conclusion form, you'd have to write:

> The Bible is true, because God wrote it.
>
> The Bible says that God exists.
>
> Therefore, God exists.

To defend the claim that the Bible is true, the arguer claims that God wrote it. But, obviously, if God wrote the Bible, He exists. Thus the argument *assumes* just what it is trying to prove.

complex question: posing a question or issue in such a way that a person cannot agree *or* disagree with you without committing him- or herself to some other claim you wish to promote. Simple example: "Are you still as self-centered as you used to be?" Answering either "yes" *or* "no" commits you to agreeing that you used to be self-centered. More subtle example: "Will you follow your conscience, instead of your pocketbook, and donate to the cause?" Anyone who says "no," regardless of his or her real reasons for not donating, is made to feel ignoble; anyone who says "yes," regardless of his or her real reasons for donating, is made to feel noble. If you want a donation, just ask for a donation.

composition: assuming that a whole must have the properties of its parts, e.g., "Since the members of the team are fine athletes, the team must be a fine team." Even fine athletes may work poorly together. Opposite of **division**.

denying the antecedent: a deductive fallacy of the form:

> If **p** then **q**.
>
> Not-**p**.
>
> Therefore, not-**q**.

For example:

> If the roads are icy, the mail is late.
>
> The roads are not icy.
>
> Therefore, the mail is not late.

Both premises could be true and the conclusion still false. The mail may be late for other reasons besides icy roads. The argument *overlooks alternative explanations*. Notice that this fallacy resembles modus tollens; take care!

division: assuming that the parts of a whole must have the properties of the whole, e.g., "Since this is a fine team, the members of the team must be fine athletes." A group of players may work together effectively without being outstanding individual players. Opposite of **composition**.

equivocation: using a single word in more than one sense: see rule 7.

false cause: generic term for a questionable conclusion about cause and effect. Turn to rules 20–23 and try to figure out specifically *why* the conclusion is (said to be) questionable.

false dilemma: reducing the options you consider to just two, often sharply opposed and unfair to the person against whom the dilemma is posed, e.g., "America: Love it or Leave it." Here is a more subtle example from a student paper: "Since the universe could not have been created out of nothingness, it must have been created by an intelligent life-force. . . ." Is creation by an intelligent life-force the *only* other possibility? Arguing from a false dilemma is sometimes a way of not playing fair: it also, obviously, overlooks alternatives.

loaded language: see rule 5.

non sequitur: drawing a conclusion that "does not follow": i.e., a conclusion that is not a reasonable inference from the evidence. Very general term for a bad argument. Try to figure out specifically what is (supposed to be) wrong with the argument.

the "person who" fallacy: see section 10.

persuasive definition: defining a term in a way which appears to be straightforward but which in fact is subtly loaded, e.g., Ambrose Bierce, in *The Devil's Dictionary*, defines "faith" as "belief without evidence in what is told by one who speaks without knowledge, of things without parallel." Persuasive definitions may favorably loaded too: e.g., defining "conservative" as "someone with a realistic view of human limits."

petitio principii: Latin for **begging the question**.

poisoning the well: using **loaded language** to disparage an argument before even mentioning it.

> I'm confident that you haven't been taken in by those few holdouts who still haven't outgrown the superstition that ...

More subtle:

> No sensitive person thinks that ...

post hoc, ergo propter hoc (literally, "after this, therefore because of this"): assuming causation too readily on the basis of mere succession in time. Again a very general term for what Chapter V tries to make precise. Turn to Chapter V and try to figure out specifically *why* the argument assumes causation too readily.

provincialism: mistaking a local fact for a universal one. I have heard it seriously argued, for instance, that eating three meals a day is a universal human behavior.

red herring: introducing an irrelevant or secondary subject and thereby diverting attention from the main subject. Usually the red herring is an issue about which people have strong opinions, so that no one notices how their attention is being diverted. In a discussion of the relative safety of different makes of car, for instance, the issue of which cars are made domestically and which are imported is a red herring.

straw man: caricaturing an opposing view so that it is easy to refute: see rule 5.

suppressed evidence: presenting only the *part* of a piece of evidence that supports your claim while ignoring the parts that contradict your claim, e.g., excerpting just the phrase "... You must go to *Flames and Glory*" from a movie review which actually said "If you must go to *Flames and Glory*, take a book." Don't laugh: it happens.

weasel word: using a word in a way which empties it of meaning (as weasels suck the contents out of an egg while leaving the shell intact). Usually a maneuver performed under the pressure of a counterexample.

> A: All studying is torture.
>
> B: What about studying argument: you love that!
>
> A: Well, that's not really studying.

Here "studying" is the weasel word. A's response to B's objection in effect changes the meaning of "studying" to "studying which is torture": so A's first statement remains true, but only at the cost of becoming trivial ("All studying which is torture is torture."). See also the discussion of "selfish" in section 7.

Appendix

For Further Study

Argument Composition

On composition generally, Strunk and White's famous *The Elements of Style* is still unparalleled (and the discerning reader will note my own debt to Strunk and White). More generally, see Nancy Cavender and Len Weiss, *Thinking in Sentences: A Guide to Clear Writing* (New York: Houghton Mifflin, 1982) and R. Lanham, *Revising Prose* (New York: Scribner's, 1979).

On composing argumentative essays, many available books go into more detail than Chapters VI–IX of this book. Especially good is Jack Meiland's *College Thinking*, Part One. For more detail on the points in Chapter VIII in particular, see Jeanne Fahnestock and Marie Secor, *A Rhetoric of Argument* (New York: Random House, 1982), Chapter 13.

Samples and Polling

See Mildred Parten, *Surveys, Polls, and Samples* (New York: Harper & Row, 1950), and Morris J. Slonim, *Sampling* (New York: Simon & Schuster, 1960).

Arguments by Analogy

Related forms of argument are discussed very usefully in Chaim Perelman, *The Realm of Rhetoric* (Notre Dame: University of Notre Dame Press, 1982), especially in Chapters 7 and 10.

Arguments about Cause and Effect

"Mill's Methods," a somewhat formalized approach to reasoning about cause and effect, are presented in I.M. Copi, *Introduction to Logic* (New York: Macmillan, many editions), Chapter 12. More on the social-scientific use of statistical reasoning can be found in R. Rosnow and R. Rosenthal, *Essentials of Behavioral Research* (New York: Holt, Rinehart, and Winston, 1984). On causal and inductive explanations generally, useful discussions are Chapters Nine and Ten of Jerry Cederblom and Donald Paulsen's *Critical Reasoning* (second edition, Belmont, California: Wadsworth, 1986), and Larry Wright, *Better Reasoning* (New York: CBS, 1982), Chapter 3.

Deductive Arguments

Formal logic begins with the forms presented here but expands them into a symbolic system of much greater power. Many good texts are available: see, e.g., William

Gustason and Dolph Ulrich, *Elementary Symbolic Logic* (Prospect Heights, Illinois: Waveland Press, 1973).

Among other things, the forms presented in sections 24–29 cannot deal with such obviously valid arguments as

Some officeholders are untrustworthy persons.

All untrustworthy persons should be turned out of office.

Therefore, some officeholders should be turned out of office.

These are called "categorical" arguments, since they have to do with categories. Formal symbolic logic incorporates categorical arguments into a system which includes modus ponens, modus tollens, etc., too, but a simpler and somewhat independent way of dealing with them is also available. This is called the Venn diagram method after its inventor, mathematician John Venn. See, e.g., Copi's Chapter 6.

Fallacies

For a more extensive list of fallacies, with illustrations, see Howard Kahane, *Logic and Contemporary Rhetoric* (Belmont, California: Wadsworth, 4th edition, 1984). For an historical and theoretical treatment of the fallacies, see C. Hamblin, *Fallacies* (London: Methuen, 1970). For more on the common fallacies, see Richard Nisbett and Lee Ross, *Human Inference* (Englewood Cliffs, New Jersey: Prentice-Hall, 1980).